HISTORY OF PHILOSOPHY AND PHILOSOPHICAL EDUCATION

Aquinas Lecture 1947, Fall

HISTORY OF PHILOSOPHY
AND PHILOSOPHICAL
EDUCATION

Under the Auspices of the Aristotelian Society
of Marquette University

BY *Henry*

ÉTIENNE GILSON *1884-*

*of the Académie française, Professor of the
History of Mediaeval Philosophy, Pontifical
Institute of Mediaeval Studies, Toronto.*

48-1955

MARQUETTE UNIVERSITY PRESS
MILWAUKEE
1948

Nihil Obstat

Gerard Smith, S.J., censor deputatus
Milwaukiae, die 24 Decembris, 1947

Imprimatur

✠Moyses E. Kiley
Archiepiscopus Milwaukiensis
Milwaukiae, die 5 mensis Januarii, 1948

To

A. C. Pegis
Who Knows Why

PREFATORY

The Aristotelian Society of Marquette University each year invites a scholar to deliver a lecture in honor of St. Thomas Aquinas. Customarily delivered on the Sunday nearest March 7th, the feast day of the Society's patron saint, these lectures are called the Aquinas lectures.

In 1947, after Dr. Vernon Bourke delivered a lecture, "St. Thomas and the Greek Moralists," on March 9 the Society invited another scholar, whose duties do not permit him to come to the University on the customary date, to give another Aquinas lecture in the fall. It now has the pleasure of recording that lecture, given Oct. 26, by Étienne Gilson of the Académie Française.

Étienne Henri Gilson was born June 13, 1884 at Paris. He received his Agrégé in 1907 and became Docteur-ès-Lettres in 1913. At the Sorbonne he was a pupil of Lucien Levy-Bruhl who taught him historical method and suggested the study of Descartes' borrowings from Scholasticism, a work which led him to St. Thomas Aquinas and the middle ages, the principal concern of his scholarly career. He was also a pupil, at the Collége de France, of Henri Bergson, "whose lectures" he recently said "still remain in my memory as so many hours of intellectual transfiguration," and whom he calls "the only living master in philosophy" he ever had.

In 1913 he taught at the University of Lille. During the first world war he was a machine-gunnery captain in the French army, was captured at Verdun and spent his time in a German prisoner of war camp writing and studying. After the war, in

1919, he joined the faculty of the University of Strasbourg. In 1921 he returned to the Sorbonne, this time to teach, and remained there until 1932 when he was elected to the Collége de France. He is now Professor of the Philosophy of the Middle Ages at the Collége de France. In 1929 he also became Director of Studies and Professor of the History of Mediaeval Philosophy at the newly established Institute of Mediaeval Studies, Toronto, Canada, of which he is a co-founder and which in 1939 was raised to a Pontifical Institute by Pius XII. He continues in those positions now. Ordinarily, he teaches in Toronto during the fall and returns to Paris at Christmas time.

Professor Gilson has held notable lectureships. In 1930 and 1931 he gave the Gifford Lectures at the University of Aberdeen, Scotland; in 1936-37 he gave the William James lectures at Harvard; in 1937, the Richards lectures at the University of

Virginia, and in 1940, the Mahlon Powell lectures at the University of Indiana.

He is founder and director of *Archives d'Histoire Doctrinale et Littéraire du Moyen-âge* (with R.P.G. Théry) of which 16 volumes have been published since 1925; *Études de Philosophie Médiévale*, 35 volumes since 1921; *Études de Theologie et d'Histoire de la Spiritualité*, 9 volumes since 1934, and founder (with colleagues at the Pontifical Institute of Mediaeval Studies) of *Mediaeval Studies*, of which 9 volumes have been published since 1939.

Professor Gilson is a member of the French Academy, the Royal Academy of Holland, the British Academy, the American Academy of Arts and Sciences and the Pontifical Academy of St. Thomas Aquinas at Rome.

He has received many honorary degrees: Doctor of Letters (D.Litt.) from Oxford University; Doctor of Laws (LL.D.)

from the University of Aberdeen, Harvard University and the University of Pennsylvania; Doctor of Philosophy (Ph.D.) from Rome, University of Milan and the University of Montreal.

He is president of the Franco-Canadian Institute, president of the Society of Catholic Authors at Paris, a member of the Secours Catholique International and of Pax Romana, before which he has lectured in Rome.

Professor Gilson entered the Conseil de la Republique, the upper house or senate of the present French government in 1946. He was technical adviser to the French delegation to the San Francisco Conference that same year, composing the French text of the Charter of the United Nations. He was also a French delegate to UNESCO, the United Nations Educational, Scientific and Cultural Organization, for which he also wrote the French text.

Professor Gilson has published the following volumes up to December 1947:

Index scolastico-cartésien, Paris, Alcan, 1913, ix and 355 pages. Out of print.

La Liberté chez Descartes et la théologie, Paris, Alcan, 1913, 453 pages. Out of print.

Études de philosophie médiévale. Collection des travaux de la Faculté des lettres de Strasbourg, Strasbourg, 1921, viii and 291 pages. Out of print.

La Philosophie de Saint Bonaventure, Paris, Vrin, 1st edition, 1924, 420 pages; 2nd edition, 1943, 483 pages; 1st edition translated under the title of *The Philosophy of Saint Bonaventure,* Sheed & Ward, New York, 1938, xiii and 551 pages.

Discours de la Méthode (Descartes) edited with commentary, Paris, Vrin, 1st edition 1925, 2nd edition 1939, text 78, commentary 490 pages.

Saint Thomas d'Aquin, (Les moralists chrétiens) texts and commentary, Paris, Gabalda, 6th edition 1941, 380 pages, translated under the title of *Moral Values and the Moral Life,* St. Louis & London, Herder, 1931, 329 pages.

Études sur le rôle de la pensée médiévale dans la formation de système cartésien, Paris, Vrin, 1930, 345 pages.

L'Esprit de la philosophie médiévale (the Gifford lectures of 1930-31) Paris, Vrin, 1st edition, 2 vols., 1932; 2nd edition, 1 vol., 1944, 447 pages; translated under the title of *The Spirit of Mediaeval Philosophy,* New York, Scribners, 1936, 1 vol., 484 pages.

Les Idées et les Lettres, Paris, Vrin, 1932, 300 pages.

Pour un ordre catholique, Paris, Desclée de Brouwer, 1934, 237 pages.

La Théologie mystique de Saint Bernard, Paris, Vrin, 1934, 251 pages; translated under the title of *The Mystical Theology of St. Bernard,* New York, Sheed & Ward, 1940, 264 pages.

Saint Thomas Aquinas, from *Proceedings of the British Academy,* Vol. XXI, London, Humphrey Milford, 1935, 19 pages.

Le Réalisme methódique, Paris, P. Tequi, 1936, 101 pages.

Christianisme et philosophie, Paris, Vrin, 1936, 168 pages, out of print; translated under the title of *Christianity and Philosophy,* New York, Sheed & Ward, 1939, 134 pages.

The Unity of Philosophical Experience (the William James lectures of 1937) New York, Scribners, 1937, 331 pages.

Mediaeval Universalism and Its Present Value (Harvard Tercentenary Conference 1936) New York, Sheed & Ward, 1937, 22 pages.

Reason and Revelation in the Middle Ages (the Richards lectures of 1937) New York, Scribners, 1938, 110 pages.

Héloïse et Abélard, Paris, Vrin, 1938, 252 pages.

Réalisme thomiste et critique de la connaissance, Paris, Vrin, 1939, 239 pages; soon to be translated into English.

Dante et la philosophie, Paris, Vrin, 1939, x and 341 pages.

God and Philosophy (the Powell lectures of 1940) New Haven, Yale University Press, and Oxford, Oxford University Press, 1941, 144 pages.

Introduction a l'étude de Saint Augustin, Paris, Vrin, 1st edition, 1929, ii and 352 pages; 2nd edition 1943, 352 pages; soon to be translated into English.

La Philosophie au moyen-âge, Paris, Payot, 2nd edition, 1944, 763 pages, soon to be translated into English.

Théologie et histoire de la spiritualité, Paris, Vrin, 1943, 27 pages.

Le Thomisme, Paris, Vrin, 5th edition 1945, 523 pages; 3rd edition translated under the title of *The Philosophy of St. Thomas Aquinas,* St. Louis, Herder, 1941; 362 pages; 5th edition soon to be translated into English.

Philosophie et Incarnation selon Saint Augustin (Conférence Albert le Grand, 1947), Montréal, Institut D'Études Médiévales Université de Montréal, 1947, 55 pages.

L'Être et l'essence is in the process of being published by Vrin, Paris, 1948.

Being and Some Philosophers is scheduled to be published by MacMullen, New York, in 1948.

To these the Aristotelian Society takes pleasure in adding *History of Philosophy and Philosophical Education.*

HISTORY OF PHILOSOPHY AND
PHILOSOPHICAL EDUCATION

History of Philosophy and Philosophical Education

THE very name of philosophy means the love of wisdom. To philosophize, then, is to pursue wisdom through a consistent effort of reflexion, which itself entails definite ethical requirements; for indeed no man can, at one and the same time, both philosophize and indulge in such ways of life as are incompatible with philosophical thinking. Yet even supposing that these moral conditions are satisfied, the fact remains that, by its very nature, a philosopher's life is a constant effort to acquire wisdom.

But what is wisdom? According to its classical definition, it is the knowledge of the first principles and of the first causes. Of course, it includes the knowledge of many other things as well; but in so far as he is using his wisdom, a wise man knows all the rest as included in, or at least, related to the first principles and the first causes. We are not without some experience as to what this means. There are things which we know because we remember them, and there are things which we know, not because we remember them, but because we know some other things through which we can always find them again if need be, without burdening our memory with cumbersome and unnecessary details. Every time our intellect thus succeeds in substituting some principles and causes of knowledge for knowledge itself, it is on the right road to wisdom. As a matter of fact, it has already

found wisdom, at least in part, while await-
ing the day when, fully aware of what the
absolutely first principles and the first causes
truly are, it begins to see everything else in
their light.

If this be true, philosophy is less a
knowledge than a life dedicated to the pur-
suit of a definite type of knowledge, namely, wisdom. It is a rather peculiar sort of
occupation and a life-long one. This is why
there are so few philosophers, by which I
mean men whose entire lives are wholly
and ultimately dedicated to the task of
achieving wisdom. True enough, most men
are fond of saying, from time to time, that
they too are philosophers. And they are, in
their own way, inasmuch as, through a long
experience of things and men, plus a certain
amount of reflexion, they have reached
some general conclusions which they call
their philosophy. Yet they are not philoso-

phers, precisely because their so-called philosophy has grown spontaneously out of
their lives, whereas a philosopher's life is
completely dedicated to the conquest of wisdom. If one is a philosopher, he can do
nothing else than philosophize; or, if he
does something else, he will do it with a
view to securing the freedom he needs for
philosophizing. I hope I will not startle you
if, the better to make clear what I have in
mind, I say that even professors of philosophy are not philosophers. Some of them
may be, but not all, nor always. For indeed,
teaching philosophy and philosophizing are
far from being one and the same thing.

If it is thinking aloud, the teaching of
philosophy may help philosophical reflexion; but it will not help if one's teaching career is spent in repeating by rote the very
same philosophical formulas, and this
sometimes for twenty years or more. To a

truly great philosopher, teaching is a nuisance, or, at least, a lesser evil. His professorial position is to him, of all positions, the one that enables him to earn a living with the slightest possible damage to his true philosophical life. While he is teaching, he is perhaps not philosophizing, but, at least, he is talking about philosophy. Such an avocation takes him away from philosophy as little as possible. This is what Thomas Aquinas calls *contemplata aliis tradere.* Yet, when all is said and done, to teach is to act, whereas to philosophize is to contemplate, and though, in this one instance, the active life of a man is but the overflowing of his contemplative life, these two lives are not the same. Even their proximate objects are different. It is one thing, for instance, to speculate about the relations of being to becoming, and it is quite another thing to prepare twenty pupils for their final examination at the end of the year. At the very same time when Bergson was teaching first-year philosophy in college, he was engaged in writing his celebrated *Essay on the Immediate Data of Consciousness.* Yet, had he attempted to teach his pupils what he himself was personally then interested in, they would all have failed their examinations, and, however great a philosopher he might have been, he may very well have lost his job. In point of fact, those of us who have seen copy-books of his college lectures, know that his course was pretty much the same as that of any ordinary professor of philosophy. It contained sound and well ordered information about psychology, methodology, ethics and metaphysics, in accord with the requirements and the order of the French official program. Now such as it was, Bergson's course was a very good introduction to philosophy indeed; but there were many other teachers, at the very same time, who were doing exactly the same thing. It would be betraying him to publish such a course under his own name, since, as a philosopher, he had very little to do with it. I once met a captain in the French army who had been a pupil of Bergson's in those early courses. Naturally, I asked him what sort of professor Bergson was. "A wonderful one," came the answer. Then, after a brief pause, the captain added with a smile: "But, of course, we did not know he was Bergson." That is why, even though your professor of philosophy may happen to be also a philosopher, you do not know him and you do not meet him as such in your classrooms. He is a philosopher, not when he is speaking to you but during those hours of solitude when he is speaking to himself in the quietness of his own meditation.

This raises a rather puzzling problem for those who want to study philosophy and perhaps still more for those whose work it is to teach it. If philosophy is the occupation of a life time, how can it be learned or taught within three or four or five years? Should we not even ask: how can it be learned or taught at all? According to what we said a moment ago, the quest of wisdom is a personal affair. If wisdom is to be your own wisdom, then its quest must be your own quest. The fact that your teacher knows truth and tells you what it is does not mean that you know it too; but however long it takes you to realize the meaning of his words, when you do, you know truth exactly as he does, and that truth is yours exactly as his truth is his. It may be the same truth, but every one who knows it, knows it through his own intellect, so that, ultimately, he is his own teacher.

Such is, as I believe, the meaning of St. Augustine's *De Magistro,* a work whose conclusion is that no one teaches any one else anything. Yet, all over the world, pupils and students know from bitter experience that this is too good to be true. If it were true, all teachers would at once lose their jobs. They don't, or, at least, when one of them does, he is at once replaced by another one; so that, on the whole, everything happens as though teachers were, in fact, doing something. And what they do can be learned from Thomas Aquinas who, happily completing what St. Augustine has said on this point, observes that teachers, though they cannot think for us, can yet make us think for ourselves, or, at least, help us in so doing. Through carefully selected words, which are the signs of his own concepts and his own judgments, a competent teacher can give rise to similar concepts and similar judgments in the minds of his pupils. What pupils learn from their teachers is not necessarily what their teachers think; rather, it is what they understand from what their teachers say. This is where St. Augustine was right: no one can know anything except through his own mind. Yet the misunderstandings that may arise can be avoided, corrected, and finally eliminated. When a teacher has at length succeeded in making his own thought clear to one or several of his own pupils, he has not substituted his own intellect for theirs, but he has certainly taught some one something.

How, then, is the teacher going to teach philosophy? We are not here concerned with the technical details of philosophical pedagogy. Obviously, there are as many good ways of teaching philosophy as there are good professors of philosophy, and however different their ways may be, if they are good professors, their ways are all good. Our main concern at the moment is with a much wider problem: what is the best approach to philosophy? Here, again, it can be said that there are several good ones, and that what is good for some students may not be quite as good for students of a different kind. But, in the end, and even though a professor were successively to try different approaches to philosophy, he could still try them only one at a time; and the only justification he could feel in trying any one of them is that it is, or at least might be, the best approach to philosophy. Our question, therefore, remains: what is this best approach to philosophy going to be, and for what reasons shall we consider it as better than any other?

One of Descartes' friends once asked him how, according to him, his own son should be taught philosophy. To this question the philosopher made a surprising answer. He did not say: let him read my own works; he said: let your son learn philosophy as it is being taught in the schools of the Jesuits, that is, by taking the whole course in philosophy from beginning to end. Now we know very well what such philosophical courses usually are. *Cursus philosophiae, Compendium philosophiae, Elementa philosophiae, Summa philosophiae,* whatever its name, such a book is supposed to give us a general survey of philosophical problems as well as of their possible solutions. When written from the point of view of Thomas Aquinas, it becomes a *Cursus philosophiae Thomisticae,* a *Compendium philosophiae ad mentem Thomae Aquinatis,* or something of the sort. In all cases, works of this kind purport to be so many "Introductions to Philosophy," or, if they are both more clear sighted and more ambitious, they are so many "Initiations to the Philosophical Life." The striking success of this sort of philosophical literature would be unintelligible if it did not answer a genuine need. In point of fact it does. When a person asks us to describe a country, the best answer to give is to show him a map. This is not the best ultimate answer, but it is the best first one; and in so far as introductions to philosophy are concerned, their greatest merit is to be both maps of, and guides to, what still is for beginners the unknown country of philosophy.

It would be sheer folly to act otherwise. In the first place, not all those who study philosophy will become philosophers. What else do they need if not to be informed, be it in a superficial way, about its nature, its main problems and their correct solution? But even those beginners, to whom such an introduction will open the way to the true philosophical life, will later on feel thankful for having entered it in the same way. No beginner should be asked to start from scratch, as though philosophy had not begun to exist twenty-four centuries ago, and nothing had ever been said or written about it. True enough, our problem may appear somewhat more simple if what we want to do is to teach philosophy *ad mentem Thomae Aquinatis;* but it actually is not. No work of Thomas Aquinas has been written for beginners in philosophy, and when he wrote his philosophical treatises or commentaries, he himself was very far from being a beginner writing for beginners. This is so true that, from the thirteenth century down to our own day, innumerable commentaries on

St. Thomas have been written which are intended as so many introductions to the personal reading of his own works. Such are probably the reasons—or, if not these, at least similar ones—which prompted Descartes, the sworn enemy of scholastic philosophy to recommend a complete course in scholastic philosophy as the best introduction to philosophical knowledge. This was a very sound piece of advice, and one that it would be very wise to give even today.

Let us suppose, now, that such advice has been wisely given and wisely accepted. Where does this lead us? After receiving this first introduction to philosophy, some beginners will quit, and they will be by far in the majority; a few others will wish to go on, and these are the only ones in whom we should now be interested. Were they to

ask us what to do, how should we answer
them?

A first way to answer their question might
be to suggest another introduction to philosophy. For introductions are plentiful,
and no two of them are identical. Still better, after a truly elementary one, we might
suggest a series of progressively more and
more difficult introductions, until the time
comes for the student, by now no longer a
beginner, to apply to those specialized
books that deal with the particular problems which interest him. Now I am very
far from finding fault with such a pedagogical method. The only question which
concerns me is, what notion of philosophy
such a method entails. And the only answer
I can imagine is that, for those who hold
such a way of learning philosophy as wholly
satisfactory and practically self-sufficient,
philosophy probably appears as a science

essentially similar to other sciences and hence capable of being taught in exactly the same way. Is not a science a body of cognitions related to the same object, rationally demonstrable and therefore communicable by means of teaching? Such are, for instance, mathematics, physics, chemistry and biology. And one fails to see for what reason philosophy, if it is a science, should not likewise be taught and learned as are the other sciences, that is to say, through introducing beginners to its problems, its methods and its present conclusions.

The better to answer this question, let us ask another one. In what sense is such a pedagogical method the proper way to teach the sciences? The ready answer is: to the full extent to which a science is made up of already acquired results. You can learn physics from oral lectures or from printed text books; but even after personally check-

ing your thus acquired learning by conduct-
ing suitable experiments in the laboratory,
what are you fitted to become? Perhaps a
useful engineer, or a good professor of
physics; but a physicist, *no*. A learned man
conversant with science, *yes*. But a scientist,
no. Professors of history may well know a
great deal of history, they may all be scholars,
yet very few of them are historians.   So,
too, we may come to know a great deal
about the physics or the philosophy of
our time without necessarily being either
physicists or philosophers. As with introductions to the other sciences, so in the case
of philosophy: where philosophy begins,
introductions to philosophy should come to
an end. What then begins, if it is to begin
at all, is a really new experience, something
as radically different from what went before it as being a great professor of English
literature is different from being a Shake-

speare. Not merely to learn philosophy, but to become a philosopher, this is what is now at stake. It does not involve giving up philosophy as a science; it rather involves aiming at possessing philosophy in a different and more exalted way as included in wisdom itself, to which it is in the same relation as a body to its soul. Then also does the philosophical life truly begin, and its beginning does not consist in any addition to already acquired learning; it rather looks like falling in love, like answering the call of a vocation, or undergoing the transforming experience of a conversion.

I am not here describing the self-revelation of some powerful genius, nor the birth of a great philosopher, whose writings will later be considered as a landmark in the field of philosophy. One cannot create in philosophy unless he be a true philosopher; but one can live and die a true philosopher without having created anything philosophical. Without his creative genius, a great philosopher would remain at least a philosopher. The difference, however, which I am trying to describe is less to be found in some exceptional quality of the mind than in its desire to achieve an active and personal appropriation of philosophical truth. In the mind of a man born to the philosophical life, ideas do not merely follow one another, be it in logical sequence, as they do when we read them for the first time in a book; they are not simply associated by the process of reasoning and the demands of demonstration; they do not merely fall into place as so many pieces of a cleverly contrived puzzle, but one would rather say that they blend into an organic whole, quickened from within by a single life and able spontaneously to assimilate or reject the spiritual food offered to it, according to the laws of its own inner development.

Whether he be destined to be great or to remain unknown within the rank and file, a philosopher once born has still to grow. He still needs to be taught, not this time philosophy, but to philosophize. And who can help him in his need, if not another philosopher who will be for him both a master and a companion during his whole life? The most urgent of all problems, then, is to find such a man, and this is far from easy; for in order to be a master, a philosopher should be great, and great philosophers are scarce. Very large countries, like Russia, have never seen one; and how many have been born, since the discovery of America, between Alaska and Patagonia? Not every Plato can hope to find his own Socrates, nor every Aristotle his own Plato. During the whole French eigh-

teenth century, the so-called "century of
philosophers," there was not a single great
philosopher.

Nor does the problem stop here. Is
not a certain spiritual affinity required between master and disciple? If in order to
learn how to walk, we need to follow someone, at least for a time, it is useless for us
to find a guide who can show us how to
do it, unless both of us wish to walk down
the same road. Some persons find it hard
to discover a religious director of conscience, yet there are no cases where the
thing cannot be done. Finding among our
contemporaries a philosophical director of
conscience is infinitely harder still; so much
so that, however anxiously a man may
search, there are many places and times
when, for him, such a discovery is absolutely impossible.

Yet, on second thought, such advisers are many and always at hand, if not in the present, at least in the past; and since we are dealing with philosophy, what difference is there between past and present? Of their very nature, metaphysics and ethics deal with problems that wholly escape time. Twenty-four centuries ago, it had already been said that being is and non-being is not; that what undergoes becoming and change does not truly deserve to be said to be; that the two foundations of society are justice and friendship, because without justice friendship is blind, just as without friendship justice is sterile. Of these three propositions, is there a single one which, during the last twenty-four centuries, has for a single moment ceased to be true? If our own contemporaries fail us, therefore, let us look into the past for the master that we need. Perhaps he is there, patiently waiting for us to tell him our own troubles and ask him our own questions. Why should we hesitate? No intelligible relation between any two terms ever belongs in the past; every time it is understood, it is in the present.

This is also the point at which the history of philosophy enters the picture as part and parcel of philosophical education— that is, provided the professors of philosophy allow history to come in. Many do not, and not without some appearance of justification. I have heard some say that the goal of a truly philosophical education is, not to know what other men have thought in the past, but what a man should think now. And there are others who will say that the history of philosophy is but the common graveyard of dead philosophies, and that living philosophers should let the dead bury their dead. Yet there is a more serious objection. It is many centuries now since Cicero said that there is nothing so foolish and so vain which has not been said by some philosopher. Descartes, who hated history under all its forms, was fond of quoting this saying; whence many professors of philosophy conclude that teaching the history of philosophy amounts to nothing more than teaching a comprehensive collection of all possible errors. Now, to teach philosophy is, or at least should be, something very different; it should be nothing less than the teaching of philosophical truth. Perhaps it might be useful to quote erroneous positions in order to refute them, but why should we invite a young and inexperienced mind to lose itself in such a forest of errors? If we know that Spinoza and Hegel were wrong, why should we let the young student read Spinoza and Hegel? We might as well feed him poison. However this may be, one thing at least is certain, and it is that the history of philosophy cannot but breed philosophical scepticism. Thus tossed without sail or wheel on a sea of conflicting opinions, a well-made mind can do but one thing with philosophy, and that is to give it up as a bad job.

I have no intention of dismissing these objections as weak or irrelevant. They are strong and very much to the point, but to theirs, not ours. They all derive their strength from the same notion of philosophy, conceived as a ready-made science, whose results have to be taught. Now, as has already been said, there is such a science, and since it should be both learned and taught, the only way to do it is the way that befits any science, namely, the dogmatic way. If a man does not think he knows what is true and what is not true in philosophy, he has no business to teach it.

As a matter of fact, many do, but they should not; and I suppose we would all agree that just as to teach physics is to teach true physics, so to teach philosophy is to teach true philosophy. It would be a very foolish thing indeed to introduce young minds to philosophy through the indiscriminate reading of texts which they cannot understand or, if they do, against which they are defenseless—as we all are in those discussions in which, wholly ignorant of the business at hand, we experience the uneasy feeling that the last speaker is always right.

But this is not at all our problem. What we are now looking for is a master, a companion and a guide in our own philosophical quest of wisdom, and because we fail to find one in the present we have to turn to the past. Thus did once the *Altissimo poeta,* when seeing himself without any one who could teach him to become a poet, he went

back more than a thousand years and found
Vergil. We do not need to go as far back
as that in order to find Thomas Aquinas.
Yet, when we meet him at long last, where
do we find him if not in history? And how
can we approach him, except through history?

Here, as I believe, is the very root of
most of our misunderstandings concerning
the proper approach to philosophy. Let us
consider this simplest of all cases. After
looking for help, some one reaches the conclusion that the best thing to do is apply to
Thomas Aquinas. He thus becomes a disciple of Thomas Aquinas, and to that extent a Thomist. So far so good. But how
does he know that he is a Thomist?

Should we ask him the question, his first
answer might be: "I know I am a Thomist
because I am in agreement with what is
written in a book in which philosophy is

taught *ad mentem Divi Thomae Aquinatis.*"
And the answer may happen to be right, but
then, how does he know that what his book
describes as the philosophy of Thomas
Aquinas is a faithful rendering of Thomas'
own thought? Obviously, the only way to
make sure is to compare such a work with
those of Thomas Aquinas himself. But just
as soon as you undertake to do this, you find
yourself engaged in straight historical work.
True enough, history is not here your goal.
What you ultimately want to know is truth,
but since your immediate problem is to
know if what Thomas Aquinas says is true,
what you first must know is what Thomas
Aquinas actually says. Nor would it do to
object that, so long as what is in the book
is true, you don't care whether Thomas
Aquinas said it or not; for this would
simply mean that you are not a disciple of
Thomas Aquinas, but of some one else free-

ly using his name. No philosopher can know that he is a Thomist unless he also be an historian.

This first conclusion is rich in many implications, which it would be tedious to enumerate. For indeed, the only man who can tell us exactly what Thomas Aquinas has said, is Thomas Aquinas himself. In order to know what he said we must read his works. But what works has he actually written? Where are the best manuscripts? In these best manuscripts, what are, according to all probabilities, the safest readings? Once we feel reasonably sure of his text, what does that text mean? Many and voluminous commentaries have been written on the Thomistic texts, but they do not always agree, and, in some cases, they seriously disagree. Now, if we have made up our minds that Thomas Aquinas found the true road to wisdom, we need to know where his road lies. We are like people following some one in a crowd because they know that he is going where they wish to go, and yet always wondering where he is. It is a hard task to find him, a still harder one not to lose him, and it is the historian's task. No wonder that so many philosophers decline to have anything to do with it. Why should they? Perhaps they need no master, no companion, no guide. My only point is that unless they resort to history, they have no right to say they are following a guide and that the name of their guide is Thomas Aquinas.

But these are minor points because, after all, they are mainly material and, so to speak, external to our problem. That problem is to know why, if Thomas Aquinas is to be our guide, he alone can do it and no one else in his place. Now let us see what may actually happen when works *ad mentem*

Divi Thomae are substituted for those of the Angelic Doctor. I am not here planning to debate any issue and take sides in it; I rather want to show that there may be very big issues involved, and that unless we walk carefully we may find ourselves miles away from our chosen guide and actually following another one who is taking us where we do not wish to go.

If there is a fundamental notion in any philosophy, it is that of being. As one conceives being, so one will conceive metaphysics. Now there is a very simple experiment which anyone can easily perform, provided only that some good philosophical library be at hand. All you need to do is to take off the library shelves some textbooks of philosophy *ad mentem Divi Thomae.* You then open these books, one by one, to the chapter that deals with the relation between essence and existence. It will not take you very much time to discover that these books fall into two classes, namely, those which affirm that there is a distinction of essence and existence *in re,* and those which deny it. In other words, according to some of these text books, the world is made up of real essences, whose existence is either a mode or some other determination, while, according to the rest, the world is made up of essences actualized by a higher act, which is the act of existing. Here are two philosophically different worlds, for indeed beings cannot, at one and the same time be essences actualized by distinct acts of existing, and essences not so actualized. What, then, is supreme in reality, essence or existence? What is supreme, *what* it is, or *that* it is? Obviously, a philosopher is here bound to make a choice; the only thing that is not possible is to maintain that there is a philosophy in which both of these views are true at one and the same time. In point of fact, the authors of philosophies *ad mentem Divi Thomae* have no hesitation in making their own choices, but these choices contradict one another—and yet their authors are all Thomists. Now I shall not here tell you what my own choice would be, or, rather, what my own choice is. I could not possibly do so because it would be sheer arbitrariness to state it, while to justify it would involve us in endless historical demonstrations. But one thing, at least, is sure. It is this: whichever of the two parties to this discussion is right, the other one is wrong. Through their wilful neglect of history, many philosophers profess publicly to follow a certain leader and then actually follow another one; which is a refreshing spectacle, well suited to bringing poor historians some consolation.

This slightly ludicrous confusion, however, would not mean very much if the mistake about names which it implies did not presuppose a more serious mistake about things. Whoever is here committing an error, it is a fact that he is mistaken about the very nature of philosophy itself; and, strangely enough, his mistake has, once again, something to do with the practical requirements of teaching in schools. A historical example will perhaps make clearer what I have in mind. In the early decades of the nineteenth century, there existed an official government program for French faculties of philosophy. It was a very simple one: the doctrine to be taught by them was that of Locke, with all suitable corrections. Now my question is this: does this make sense? I am very much afraid that, to a very large number of professors of philosophy it does make sense, and I almost despair of making clear why it does not. For, as a matter of fact, that is what everybody has to do if he is called on to give a course in philosophy. Whether the philosopher whom he is following be Thomas Aquinas, Duns Scotus, Locke, Kant or Royce does not make much difference as concerns our own problem. For the trouble is that, being professors of philosophy, we have to extract lecture courses in general philosophy out of the works of philosophers, who have themselves never written any such thing. The nearest approach to it is the work of Aristotle, whose encyclopedic nature is one of the many reasons why, at all times and in all places, his philosophy has been so highly prized by university professors. Yet even to Aristotle, philosophy was his philosophy, just as to Locke philosophical truth was identical with the views laid down in his *Essay on Human Understanding.* As an expression of a single organic thought, a philosopher's personal philosophy enjoys an organic unity of its own, which makes it difficult, not to say impossible, to expand or to curtail it, to correct or to remodel it, with a view to bringing it up to date and to adapting it to the requirements of modern classroom teaching. If, in Locke's philosophy, you correct any one of those consequences which follow necessarily from his principles, you are, in fact, denying his principles and rejecting his philosophy. When, in the early thirteenth century, the teaching of Aristotle's writings was forbidden *donec corrigantur,* it soon became apparent that they would never be corrected. They could not be. It was then that Thomas Aquinas did the only thing that it was possible to do: he created a new philosophy, which would have staggered Aristotle had

he known it, since it was no longer his philosophy but that of Thomas Aquinas.

Such is, as I see it, the fundamental distinction that we should always observe between a text book in philosophy and a
philosophical treatise. Each of them serves
its own purpose, but their purposes are not
the same. A text book in philosophy, or
even any course of lectures written as a
text book, is bound to lack that organic
unity and continuity of thought which
marks the works of authentic philosophical
reflexion. Wondering about the difference
between genius and talent in music, Robert
Schumann once came to the conclusion that
in all works of genius there is a golden
thread running throughout the whole and
holding it together. This, no doubt, is the
reason why another musician, Igor Stra-
vinski, does not like to be called a "com-
poser," nor his works "compositions." And

so it is also with philosophy. Even when they are not compiled, textbooks are composed, whereas philosophies are born.

There is only one way to prove this, but no one can prove it to anyone else, for the proof lies in a personal experience which history alone can give. The proof lies in a life spent in personal and intimate contact with great philosophers. Of all those who have learned philosophy only in schools or from books written only for schools I am sorry to say that they have not the slightest idea of what the philosophical life really is. Not unlike the innumerable students who spend years in learning Latin and never use it to read Vergil, our students in philosophy are introduced to a philosophical life which very few of them will ever enter. I cannot help wondering, however, if a larger number among them would not enjoy living a genuinely philosophical life, if they were warned in due time that what we must teach them as philosophy is not yet philosophy, but a way to it, and that the only true masters in philosophy there are, are the great philosophers?

For those at least among our students who have heard the call of philosophy and are eager to answer it, how could we have the slightest hesitation? What are we, professors of philosophy, if not students older than our own students? We cannot be their masters, since we are not masters. When our work with them has been completed, let us take them directly to him who is our own master. Let us, henceforth, teach them to learn with him, and under him, not with us and under us. True enough, we can still help them, but not as before. Our new task is to teach them to learn from one greater than ourselves, to read Thomas Aquinas, to assimilate his thought, to think with him as a true philosopher does, that is with the same standard of scientific objectivity and accuracy, until the time comes when the whole body of his doctrine will appear to them shot through with the light of its first principles. When will that time come? No one can tell, but certainly not before many years of study, for there is no short road to riches in philosophy. Yet come it will, and when it does philosophy will shine before their eyes in the purity of its essence. And because a greater than we are will have enabled them to share in its life, they shall not fail to recognize in it the true source of its intelligible beauty, Wisdom that "reacheth from end to end mightily and ordereth all things sweetly." (*Wis.* VIII, 1)

That is why, unless I be greatly mistaken, the history of philosophy should be recognized everywhere as an essential part of a complete philosophical education.

By this I mean an education whose ultimate goal is, not to teach philosophy but to form full-fledged philosophers. And just as in the case of everything else that is good, there is a price that we must pay, so, too, here; but the price is worth paying. At any rate, that price is not what it is said to be by those professors of philosophy who, in their ill-advised zeal for pure abstract speculation, seek to frighten us away from historical studies. Even supposing, *dato non concesso,* that all their intentions are always wholly pure, their reasons would still not be valid, since they completely miss the point. The history of philosophy cannot be a graveyard for dead philosophers, because in philosophy there are no dead. Owing to history, all great philosophers are still alive, and none of them is showing signs of greater vitality than our master, companion and guide, St. Thomas Aquinas. Nor is the history of philosophy a school for scepticism. Quite the contrary. If there is a source of philosophical scepticism to be found anywhere, I would rather look for it in the fatal illusion shared in and widely spread by us, the professors of philosophy, that our introductions to the life of wisdom are themselves wisdom. The life of wisdom is not to be found in them, the golden thread of true philosophical thinking does not run, unbroken, through their many parts, and those of our students who carry them into life as dearly cherished treasures should be ready for a distressing experience. Under the first serious shock, the roughly sown parts of their philosophical patchquilt are bound to pull asunder. The very best thing that can then happen is that, in despairing of philosophy, they remember that God did not choose to save men through metaphysics, so that its loss be not their loss.

Would it not be more simple to clear up, once and for all, the misunderstandings that are here the source of so many problems? Neither as science nor as wisdom is philosophy to be found outside some mind of which it is a perfection, but which is its cause. Philosophy has no existence of its own outside philosophers, and even that superhuman wisdom which transcends time is given to us in time. Such also is our own wisdom in so far as we have one; such were the wisdoms of Plato, of Aristotle and of Thomas Aquinas. Like men themselves, philosophies pass away, going the way of all flesh. By a curious illusion, we like to imagine that there is somewhere in this world a philosophy subsisting in itself and for itself, of which all philosophers are equally invited to partake and in which they freely share. Why not, then, go a little farther and imagine it as laid down in such

books as contain, not the philosophy of
Plato, of Aristotle, or of Thomas Aquinas,
that is, not someone's philosophy, but philosophy pure and simple?

We may try, but the trouble is that philosophy pure and simple is a pure and simple essence, not a being. If *ens* means *habens
esse,* a philosopher is a being, whereas philosophy is not. Exactly, the only actual being
which philosophy may have is that of the
philosopher, so that the anonymity of philosophy points less to its universality than
to its lack of actual entity. What makes
philosophical truth to be universal is something quite different. For each and every
one of us, the root of what is universal in
him is identical with the very core of his
own personality. Through his intellect, every man is a person and through the same
intellect he can see exactly the same truth
as any other man can see, provided they

both use their intellects in the proper way. Here, and nowhere else, lies the foundation for the very possibility of a *philosophia perennis;* for it is, not a perennial cloud floating through the ages in some metaphysical stratosphere, but the permanent possibility for each and every human being to actualize an essence through his own existence, that is to experience again the same truth in the light of his own intellect. And that truth itself is not an anonymous one. Even taken in its absolute and self-subsisting form, truth in itself bears a name. Its name is God.

Once these fantasies are dispelled, there is room for a solid, consistent and consoling reality. We should, no doubt, grant that if there is no ready-made philosophy to teach and to learn, wisdom is the prize, not only of a quest, but also of a conquest. We all have to win it the hard way. Yet, in our

ny cen-
at leads
hen also
each its
hical re-
has been
ie. There
iving of
1 act and
ence. In
both old

1 lending
3 experi-
ay human
are of his
e smallest
wn small-
est among
ess. Is an
nber how

is alone. At the
e up the mirage
sophy, we find
ne friendly com-
They are all here,
eady to assist us
hat we apply to
they have said,
be of assistance
as himself once
very failures.
ophy looks for
osophy, but its
not find it any-
being himself
1 finds it in the
He may make
ng their num-
particularly be-
eels and soon
osopher of his

choice embarked before him, m
turies ago, upon the only path t
whither he himself wishes to go. ᵀ
does the history of philosophy
own end and find its own philoso;
ward. A new philosophical life
kindled by another philosophical li
is nothing here to suggest the ;
some gift; rather, an act answers a
an existence echoes another exi:
such a spiritual birth, everything i
and new, in time and out of time

What is there for us to lose ;
ourselves to such a transformir
ence? It is beyond the power of a
master to add an inch to the stat
disciples. But he can make even tl
among them fulfill at least their c
ness, just as he can help the great
them to achieve their own great
example necessary? Do but reme

much time and toil Thomas Aquinas has spent in commenting upon the writings of Aristotle. That work was, at one and the same time, history of philosophy pure and simple, as well as the effort of a disciple asking guidance from his master. Aristotle was the master, for every time he said *The Philosopher,* Thomas Aquinas meant Aristotle. Yet so little did his apprenticeship hamper the personal genius of the disciple, that were we asked today: Who is *the* Philosopher? we would unhesitatingly answer: Thomas Aquinas.

THE AQUINAS LECTURES

Published by the Marquette University Press,
Milwaukee 3, Wisconsin

St. Thomas and the Life of Learning (1937) by the
late Fr. John F. McCormick, S.J., professor of
philosophy at Loyola University.

St. Thomas and the Gentiles (1938) by Mortimer J.
Adler, Ph.D., associate professor of the philosophy of law, University of Chicago.

St. Thomas and the Greeks (1939) by Anton C.
Pegis, Ph.D., president of the Pontifical Institute
of Mediaeval Studies, Toronto.

The Nature and Functions of Authority (1940) by
Yves Simon, Ph.D., professor of philosophy,
University of Notre Dame.

St. Thomas and Analogy (1941) by Fr. Gerald B.
Phelan, Ph.D., director of the Mediaeval Institute,
University of Notre Dame.

St. Thomas and the Problem of Evil (1942) by
Jacques Maritain, Ph.D., French Ambassador to
the Holy See.

First in series (1937) $1.00; all others $1.50.

Humanism and Theology (1943) by Werner Jaeger, Ph.D., Litt.D., "university" professor, Harvard University.

The Nature and Origins of Scientism (1944) by Fr. John Wellmuth, S.J., chairman of the Department of Philosophy, Xavier University.

Cicero in the Courtroom of St. Thomas Aquinas (1945) by the late E. K. Rand, Ph.D., Litt.D., LL.D., Pope Professor of Latin, *emeritus,* Harvard University.

St. Thomas and Epistemology (1946) by Fr. Louis-Marie Régis, O.P., Th.L., Ph.D., director of the Albert the Great Institute of Mediaeval Studies, University of Montreal.

St. Thomas and the Greek Moralists (1947, Spring) by Vernon J. Bourke, Ph.D., professor of philosophy, St. Louis University, St. Louis, Mo.

History of Philosophy and Philosophical Education (1947, Fall) by Étienne Gilson of the *Académie française,* director of studies and professor of the history of mediaeval philosophy, Pontifical Institute of Mediaeval Studies, Toronto.

Uniform format, cover and binding.